Spotlight on Social Justice

FROM SILENCE TO SOLIDARITY

THE FIGHT FOR LGBTQ+ RIGHTS

EMILY STARBUCK GERSON

TF CB

TWENTY-FIRST CENTURY BOOKS / MINNEAPOLIS

This book is dedicated to my wife Jamie, who gave me the courage to live authentically and inspires me daily, and our families, who love us just as we are.

Twenty-First Century Books™
An imprint of Lerner Publishing Group, Inc.
241 First Avenue North
Minneapolis, MN 55401 USA

For reading levels and more information, look up this title at www.lernerbooks.com.

Main body text set in Bembo Std Regular
Typeface provided by Monotype Typography.

Library of Congress Cataloging-in-Publication Data

Names: Starbuck Gerson, Emily, author.
Title: From silence to solidarity : the fight for LGBTQ+ rights / Emily Starbuck Gerson.
Description: Minneapolis : Twenty-First Century Books, [2025] | Series: Spotlight on social justice | Includes bibliographical references and index. | Audience: Ages 11–18 | Audience: Grades 7–9 | Summary: "More North Americans are LGBTQ+ than ever before. This community has made much progress toward achieving equal rights, but many members have and continue to face legal, social, and cultural challenges. From past to present, learn about the fight for LGBTQ+ rights in North America"—Provided by publisher.
Identifiers: LCCN 2024010699 (print) | LCCN 2024010700 (ebook) | ISBN 9798765627198 (library binding) | ISBN 9798765662571 (paperback) | ISBN 9798765659502 (epub)
Subjects: LCSH: Gay rights—History—Juvenile literature. | Homophobia—History—Juvenile literature. | Gay people—Political activity—Juvenile literature. | Gay liberation movement—History—Juvenile literature.
Classification: LCC HQ76.5 .S73 2025 (print) | LCC HQ76.5 (ebook) | DDC 323.3/264—dc23/eng/20240409

LC record available at https://lccn.loc.gov/2024010699
LC ebook record available at https://lccn.loc.gov/2024010700

Manufactured in the United States of America
1 – CG – 12/15/24

CONTENTS

INTRODUCTION

The LGBTQ+ community in North America has gained significant acceptance and rights in the 2020s compared to decades and centuries ago. But what does LGBTQ+ mean?

LGBTQ+ is an inclusive acronym describing people whose sexual and romantic orientations and gender identities are diverse and varied. LGBTQ+ people are not straight (when someone is only attracted to the gender opposite their own). They also may not be cisgender or cis (when someone's gender identity, such as woman or man, corresponds with their sex assigned at birth, such as female or male).

The plus sign in the LGBTQ+ acronym means it includes even more ways people identify. The acronym may be shortened to LGBT. Or some people might add extra letters to include more identities, such as in LGBTQIA+.

The acronym can also vary by country. Some countries use LGBTQI+. Canada's government currently uses 2SLGBTQI+, which includes Two-Spirit people. *Two-Spirit* is a term for Indigenous peoples who identify as having both a male and female spirit. It can be like a third gender, and some Indigenous people use it to describe their sexual, gender, and spiritual identities. It is at the start of the acronym because Indigenous peoples made up the first communities.

Many people have adopted the word *queer* to broadly describe the entire LGBTQ+ community. But *queer* was once a slur used against LGBTQ+ people, and some people still consider it to be one. Even though it's become more popular and accepted, it's important not to assume everyone is comfortable with that label.

Another label, *homosexual*, isn't used much anymore. It traditionally means gay or lesbian but can refer to anyone in a same-sex relationship. This book uses it only when discussing older policies and laws that used that language at the time.

There are millions of LGBTQ+ people worldwide. Studies show that around 10 percent of North American adults identify as LGBTQ+.

The LGBTQIA+ Acronym

Here's what the LGBTQIA+ acronym stands for. When the community uses gendered terms such as *men* or *women*, it includes trans people who identify that way.

- **L** **Lesbian**: Women and nonbinary people who are only attracted to other women and nonbinary people.
- **G** **Gay**: Men who are only attracted to other men. People of other identities have also adopted this as an umbrella term, so it may not be used exclusively for men.
- **B** **Bisexual**: People attracted to more than one gender.
- **T** **Transgender**: People whose gender identity does not correspond with their sex assigned at birth.
- **Q** **Queer**: A broad term meaning different things. It generally indicates that the person isn't straight. Some people may use it to indicate they're not cisgender. Others may use the Q for *questioning*, meaning they're unsure about their sexual, romantic, or gender identity.
- **I** **Intersex**: People who are born with differences in sex traits, such as internal reproductive anatomy, external genitalia, chromosomes, or hormones. It's a medical condition causing variances that aren't strictly biologically male or female. There's a large variety of intersex conditions, and it's estimated around 2 percent of people are intersex. Intersex isn't a gender identity or sexual orientation. But this community is included in the LGBTQIA+ umbrella since intersex people and LGBTQ+ people share issues including accessing hormones, potentially questioning their gender identity, and having bodily autonomy. For example, intersex people historically have been subjected to surgeries as babies to make them physically "fit" a binary mold of male or female.

A Asexual: People who don't experience sexual attraction or only do so in certain situations. Some people may also use the A to include agender (people who don't identify with any gender) and aromantic (people who don't experience romantic attraction or only do in specific situations) identities.

+ Plus: People whose identities fall under the LGBTQIA+ umbrella but are not represented by a letter in the acronym, such as nonbinary (when someone doesn't identify strictly as a man or woman) or pansexual (when someone is attracted to all genders).

The rainbow flag is a symbol of LGBTQIA+ pride and solidarity. In 1978 artist Gilbert Baker designed the flag in response to a need for a symbol that could represent the LGBTQIA+ community.

What terms people prefer can be generational. For example, an older person who was bullied with the word *queer* might not embrace that label like a younger person without those negative experiences. Or they might still be comfortable with the word *homosexual*, while a younger person may find that label off-putting. What's considered acceptable or respectful can also vary across countries and cultures.

That means we can't be sure how someone would identify today when looking at the past. For example, the word *transgender* wasn't around centuries ago. If we see a historical figure who was assigned female at birth but dressed as a man, someone today might assume they're transgender. Not only did that word not exist then, but society was different. The person might have identified as a man. However, it's also possible they identified as a woman but presented as a man so they and their female partner could blend in with their conservative society or for any other reason.

The original pride flag had eight colors, each with its own meaning. Pink represents sexuality, red symbolizes life, orange represents healing, yellow stands for sunlight, green depicts nature, turquoise symbolizes creativity, indigo represents harmony, and violet symbolizes spirit. There are more than fifty different LGBTQ+ flags, and they all have their own meanings too.

CHAPTER ONE

In the Shadows

While the LGBTQ+ community has been in the spotlight more in the twenty-first century, these identities are far from new or just a trend. Historically, most LGBTQ+ people have been forced to remain closeted or live on the fringes of society due to social stigma, discriminatory laws, censorship, and cherry-picked religious dogma. In the early twentieth century, it was more common for people to think that members of the LGBTQ+ community had a mental illness. Doctors sometimes used a harmful and ineffective practice called conversion therapy to try to make LGBTQ+ people "normal." Conversion therapy still happens sometimes, but it's less prevalent, and most mainstream medical experts don't condone it.

It might be hard to imagine that being gay or trans could also land you in jail, but in the past it was the reality, and not just in North America. Two examples are Oscar Wilde and Alan Turing, two British men who were gay when it was illegal and were prosecuted for it despite being national heroes.

Oscar Wilde, Alan Turing, and Others

Born in 1854, Irish writer Wilde was lauded for his plays and books until he was arrested for being homosexual in 1895. He was jailed for two years, which is said to have broken his spirit. He died at the age of forty-six in a self-imposed exile in Europe. Turing was a gay man born in London in 1912. A mathematics and computer genius, his work helped crack codes vital to the Allied powers' victory in World War II (1939–1945). Soon after the war, he was arrested for being homosexual. Turing's arrest was thought to be a contributing factor to his death by suicide in 1954.

Some cultures of the past and present have been far more accepting. For example, it was common for ancient Greek and Roman men to have gay relationships. Additionally, for thousands of years, some communities worldwide have existed outside binary gender norms, often as third genders. Some of these include Mexico's Muxe community, India's Hijra community, Hawaii's Māhū community, and North America's Indigenous Two-Spirit communities.

But, as in the cases of Wilde and Turing, many LGBTQ+ people throughout history have faced discrimination and lacked safety and acceptance. Because of this, many historical peoples' LGBTQ+ identities have only been suspected or revealed much later. Albert Cashier was assigned female at birth in Ireland in 1843, then immigrated to the US and lived as a man. He enlisted in the military and served in the US Civil War (1861–1865), keeping his identity secret until nearly the end of his life. Many scholars believe that he would identify as a transgender man today.

First Lady Eleanor Roosevelt was long suspected to be LGBTQ+. Researchers in the 2010s found that she had a

Turing was unapologetic about his sexuality before and after his arrest. He believed that laws criminalizing homosexuality were unfair.

lengthy relationship with her close female friend, journalist Lorena Hickok, starting in 1932.

General Casimir Pulaski was born in Poland in 1745 and was assigned male at birth. He lived as a man and enlisted in the military after moving to America. Researchers who found his skeleton in the 1990s were surprised that it appeared biologically female. In the late 2010s scientific advances in DNA analysis revealed that Pulaski was likely intersex.

Queer Coding

In the past, when LGBTQ+ people couldn't live as openly, it was hard to find friends or love interests. With no social media, Internet, or Pride events, how did LGBTQ+ people find each other? The community often relied on queer coding—subtle forms of communicating one's identity that the general public wouldn't recognize. People could express their identity through language, symbols, and dress. For example, centuries ago, certain color flowers symbolized different identities, and some LGBTQ+ people in America in the 1970s and 1980s wore handkerchiefs of specific colors to signal their sexuality.

Targeted

While stories like Wilde's and Turing's may seem surprising now, it's important to recognize how LGBTQ+ people have been persecuted on a large scale throughout recent history. Most people learn in school that Hitler and Nazi Germany committed genocide against six million Jewish people during World War II, also imprisoning many of them in concentration camps. What's less frequently discussed is that he also directed the Nazis to target other communities he believed were inferior or dangerous to Nazi Germany's goals. In addition to Jews, the Nazis imprisoned and murdered people who were LGBTQ+, disabled, Black, Slavic, Roma or Sinti, political opponents, Jehovah's Witnesses, and more.

Nazis forced Jews to wear yellow stars to reflect the Star of David. They also had a labeling system for some other targeted groups. Gay men had to wear upside-down pink triangles. Those who were Jewish and gay had stars with one

Rudolf Brazda was the last known person sent to a concentration camp for his sexuality during the Holocaust. He died at the age of ninety-eight in 2011.

yellow and one pink triangle. The LGBTQ+ community has since reclaimed the pink triangle as a symbol of pride and liberation.

After the war, the US celebrated victory over the Nazis and their allies. But LGBTQ+ Americans didn't enjoy new freedoms at home. They still faced social stigma and laws that restricted and criminalized their lives.

Magnus Hirschfeld: Early leader in Global LGBTQ+ Rights

Magnus Hirschfeld was born in 1868 in then-Prussia, now part of Poland. He was a Jewish doctor devoted to researching sexuality and advocating for LGBTQ+ rights.

He believed people were born LGBTQ+ and wrote research papers about intersex and trans people. In 1897 Hirschfeld helped establish the Scientific-Humanitarian Committee, the world's first gay rights organization. In 1919 he opened the first Institute for Sexual Science in Berlin, where he and his life partner, Karl Giese, offered medical care, public education, professional training, and research.

"Soon the day will come when science will win victory over error, justice a victory over injustice, and human love a victory over human hatred and ignorance."

—Magnus Hirschfeld

Left to right: Dr. Bernhard Schapiro, Magnus Hirschfeld, and Li Shiu Tong around 1930. Schapiro taught classes at the Institute for Sexual Science. Li Shiu Tong was a pioneering researcher in bisexuality and an LGBTQ+ rights activist.

Looted books from the Institute for Sexual Science were given to Nazis to burn.

Hirschfeld's institute became a hub for the LGBTQ+ community and artists, with cutting-edge treatments, programs and events, and a public library featuring his research and writings. As the Nazis gained power, they targeted Hirschfeld and his institute, both because he was Jewish and because they thought his work and community was immoral.

Just before Hitler became Germany's Chancellor in early 1933, Hirschfeld went into self-exile in Switzerland for safety. Soon after, Nazis looted his institute and destroyed much of its archive in a massive book burning. The institute later closed completely. The organization and its priceless materials were lost. Still, Hirschfeld and his institute's legacy of accepting and affirming LGBTQ+ people will always be remembered.

The Lavender Scare

The Lavender Scare between the 1940s and 1960s began with the Red Scare following World War II, when US Senator Joseph McCarthy began hunting and persecuting suspected Communists within the US government. The imagined threat from Cold War fears ruined many careers and lives. But even as the Red Scare faded, politicians such as McCarthy whipped up paranoia about morality. They suggested that Communists and LGBTQ+ people were similar, deviant threats. A group of senators formed a committee in 1950 to investigate potential LGBTQ+ people working in the government, and the accused were forced to resign or be publicly outed.

The senators' efforts expanded, with politicians aiming to find and weed out all LGBTQ+ people working for the government, including in the military. In 1953 President Dwight D. Eisenhower signed an executive order barring LGBTQ+ people from federal government jobs, claiming they posed national security threats. It's estimated between five thousand and ten thousand people lost their jobs. In 1957 a Navy study found no security risks came from having LGBTQ+ people in the military. Still, military leadership and lawmakers who disagreed with the findings ignored them.

REFLECT

How do laws and policies continue to impact the experiences of marginalized groups such as LGBTQ+ people and communities of color? What role do laws play in creating a more unjust or fairer society?

US laws targeting homosexuality in the 1950s and 1960s led to frequent police raids and arrests in bars and restaurants where LGBTQ+ patrons gathered. Individuals were arrested for exaggerated charges to criminalize their behavior, including public displays of affection and dressing in drag. Authorities often harassed bar owners and patrons to the extent that many of these community hubs closed.

LGBTQ+ people in the US weren't the only ones facing discrimination during this period. In Canada, a long stretch starting in the 1950s was called "the LGBT Purge" since discriminatory laws targeted those in the Canadian armed forces, police forces, and federal public service. It continued until 1992, when Canada's ban on LGBTQ+ service ended.

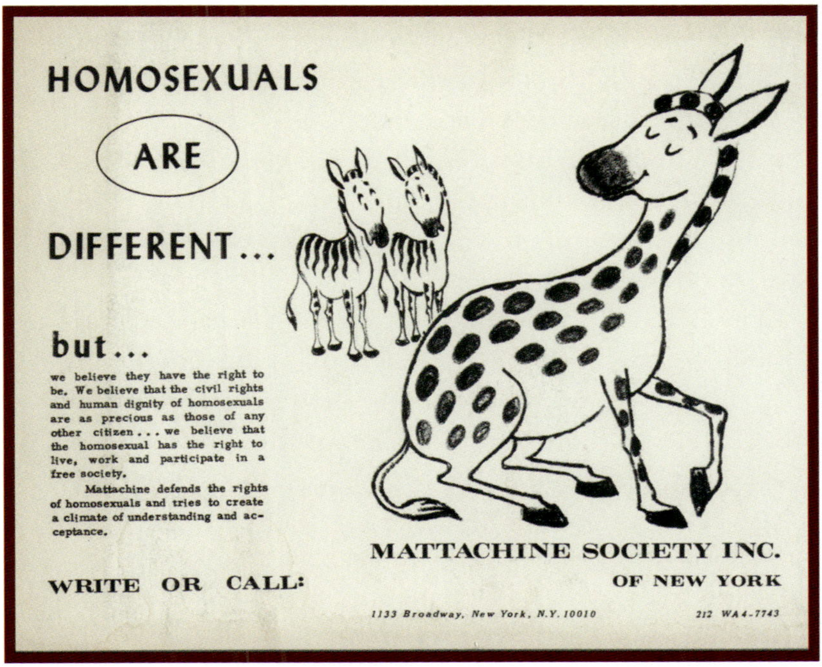

The anti-LGBTQ+ climate in the 1950s led to the formation of new LGBTQ+ organizations such as the Mattachine Society and Daughters of Bilitis. These groups fought back against discrimination.

CHAPTER TWO

Fighting for Our Rights

Amid ongoing discrimination and the momentum of the civil rights movement seeking racial equality, the 1960s ushered in intense era of LGBTQ+ activism. Legalized discrimination, social stigma, violence, and police raids continued to impact the daily lives of LGBTQ+ people, making it challenging to find work, access medical care, and have emotional stability.

The LGBTQ+ community realized they had to fight for their rights. The Stonewall Uprising, more commonly just called Stonewall, of 1969 is the best-known event. But other incidents leading up to it built traction for achieving more rights. For example, in 1965 a large sit-in occurred at Dewey's restaurant in Philadelphia, leading to the establishment's policy change to serve LGBTQ+ people.

Compton's Cafeteria Riot

A year after the Dewey's sit-in, the Compton's Cafeteria Riot unfolded in San Francisco. The city's Tenderloin District was one of the few places where trans people could openly gather. Compton Cafeteria was a 24-7 diner in Tenderloin that was a hangout for trans people, drag queens, and other LGBTQ+

In 2017 an area in the Tenderloin neighborhood became the first legally recognized transgender cultural district in the world.

people. But the police harassed patrons and arrested them for minor offenses.

In August 1966 a police officer entered Compton's Cafeteria and harassed a patron for "cross-dressing." Fed up, she resisted arrest and threw coffee in his face. Her peers joined her protest and started a riot, flipping tables and smashing plates. The protest spilled into the streets. Felicia Flames, a patron who often ate at Compton's Cafeteria in the 1960s, said about the protest, "We were tired of being arrested for nothing. Arrested for being who we wanted to be. Thrown in jail for obstructing the sidewalk. Thrown in jail for dressing like a woman because in those days it was illegal."

The riot led to positive changes and more resources in the community. For example, the continued political activism helped the area become eligible for federal support in programs such as mental health counseling, job training, and additional schools.

Stonewall

Protests, riots, demonstrations, and sit-ins continued to occur nationwide, sometimes resulting in progress. Then, on a pivotal night in June 1969, the infamous Stonewall Uprising began at the Stonewall Inn, a gay bar in New York City that police raided monthly. It had just been raided earlier that week. When the police came in for another raid, the patrons had had enough and fought back. Thousands of people joined the six days of protesting that followed, and the media covered the event.

Seeing members of the LGBTQ+ community stand up and, in some cases, achieve better treatment and legislative change motivated the rest of the community. More activist groups organized to fight oppressive discrimination. In 1970 the LGBTQ+ liberation movement formally kicked off. Activist groups worked together and partnered with related civil rights movements including those for women's rights, Black Power, anti-Vietnam War (1955–1975) efforts, and counterculture.

The events of June 1969 are also often called the Stonewall Riot, but that's inaccurate since it wasn't a one-time event. The uprising lasted for almost a week, and the persistence of those fighting for their right to exist helped usher in change.

Marsha P. Johnson & Sylvia Rivera

Many people who fought for LGBTQ+ rights were trans women and drag queens of color. Marsha P. Johnson and Sylvia Rivera were transgender women, and Johnson was also a drag queen. Johnson was Black, and Rivera was Puerto Rican and Venezuelan. These friends were among the first to join the Stonewall Uprising.

The pair became icons from their participation in Stonewall and their other activism. In 1970 they co-founded Street Transvestite Action Revolutionaries, which helped unhoused and low-income transgender people in New York City meet their basic needs.

The *P* in Marsha P. Johnson's name stood for "Pay It No Mind," which was her life motto and a response she often gave to those who questioned her gender identity.

Despite their community work, Rivera and Johnson were often shunned from the gay liberation movement, which wasn't always trans-inclusive. In 1973 Rivera wasn't allowed to speak at Gay Pride, but she grabbed the microphone to remind attendees that trans women and drag queens were on the front lines of the revolution. People booed her off stage, but she and Johnson continued their advocacy for the remainder of their lives. Their legacies live on in two organizations. The Marsha P. Johnson Institute advocates for the rights of Black transgender people, and the Sylvia Rivera Law Project provides various types of legal support and services to transgender people of color and low-income transgender people.

Activists held the first Pride March in New York City on the first anniversary of Stonewall, with an estimated ten thousand people marching. While many LGBTQ+ people now view Pride as a time to celebrate, the original goal of the event was to gather as a community and demonstrate against discriminatory laws and police treatment.

Pride has been held in New York City annually ever since, attracting millions of people around the world each year. In 1972 London held its first Pride march in June to align with the Stonewall anniversary. Many other cities, regions, states, and countries soon began hosting annual Pride events.

Some Progress

Throughout the 1970s the LGBTQ+ community still experienced significant discrimination but enjoyed some progress. In 1973 the American Psychiatric Association declared that homosexuality was no longer considered a mental illness. In 1975 well after the Lavender Scare, the US government finally made it illegal to fire federal workers for homosexuality.

Another win came in 1977 when Harvey Milk became one of America's first openly gay elected officials. Once he landed a seat on the San Francisco Board of Supervisors, which is like a city council overseeing the county, he fought for equality. He fought not only for the LGBTQ+ community but also for women and marginalized groups. He was extremely popular, attracting more attendees to Pride marches and inspiring people worldwide. Around a year after Milk took office, a former city supervisor assassinated him and San Francisco's mayor, George Moscone. The LGBTQ+

community was devastated, but Milk's legacy lives on through the Harvey Milk Foundation, which is dedicated to working toward Milk's vision.

In the next decades, Pride expanded worldwide, gradually shifting from protests for LGBTQ+ rights to celebrations with parade floats, concerts, and festivals. In 1999 US president Bill Clinton formally proclaimed June as Pride Month in the US.

Milk's activism paved the way for LGBTQ+ social progress and representation in government. He inspired change through his advocacy, community organizing, and dedication to social justice.

As Pride became more accepted, many in the LGBTQ+ community worried that the original purpose of Pride had been lost. Large companies have become staples at Pride events, with booths, sponsored events, and employees marching in parades with corporate floats. Many brands and stores also put out Pride-themed products in June. Some see this as a positive sign of mainstream acceptance. Others criticize Pride for becoming too commercial, especially since some participating companies donate to politicians who don't support the LGBTQ+ community.

Some cities launched spin-off Pride events focusing on specific communities and issues to keep in the first Pride's spirit of protesting. These include trans Pride marches, "dyke marches" led by lesbian and queer women, and Black Pride. In 2019 activists in New York City started the Queer Liberation March, which focuses on fighting for LGBTQ+ rights and celebrating LGBTQ+ history. The activists advocate for reclaiming Pride and shunning corporate and police participation.

REFLECT

Do you think corporations and police have a place at Pride events? Why or why not?

About fifty thousand people took part in 2020's Queer Liberation March. The theme of that year's march was "For Black Lives and against Police Brutality."

Intersectionality 101

Intersectionality is a framework used to explain how different facets of people's identities affect their experiences, especially with discrimination. Legal scholar and civil rights advocate Kimberlé Williams Crenshaw coined the term in 1989.

In a 2017 interview, Crenshaw explained, "Intersectionality is a lens through which you can see where power comes and collides, where it interlocks and intersects. It's not simply that there's a race problem here, a gender problem here, and a class or LGBTQ problem there. Many times, that framework erases what happens to people who are subject to all of these things."

In other words, we're complex humans not defined by just one trait. We're a unique mix of identity markers that don't operate independently, including race, class, gender identity, sexual and romantic orientation, religion, age, nationality, class, education, ability, and more. These markers intersect, and some people, particularly those with marginalized identities, then face multiple types of discrimination and oppression.

Bayard Rustin, a close advisor of Martin Luther King Jr., was outed as gay early in his career. Navigating discrimination for being Black and being gay, Rustin was a lifelong advocate for human rights.

For example, a white lesbian woman from a city will have different life experiences from one in a rural area. A Black lesbian woman will have different experiences than either, partially due to racism. A Black transgender woman navigates even more complexity and oppression. Suppose someone also has other marginalized identities, such as being Muslim or disabled. In that case, you can see how living at those intersections means they face more types of discrimination than someone with fewer marginalized identities.

CHAPTER THREE

The AIDS Crisis

In the early 1980s a new disease swept through communities of gay men in North America and, eventually, the world. Nobody knew why healthy young men were becoming ill with failing immune systems. Because of social stigma, the new illness was sometimes called "the gay plague," and governments and the medical field were accused of responding slowly due to homophobia.

Scientists soon discovered that the disease started with an infection, the human immunodeficiency virus (HIV), attacking the immune system. Eventually, HIV turned into a deadly condition, acquired immunodeficiency syndrome (AIDS). HIV was transmitted through blood, breast milk, and sexual activity. While it was mostly found in gay and bisexual men, it also infected some women, intravenous drug users, babies born to infected parents, and blood transfusion recipients.

AIDS Activism

The LGBTQ+ community stepped up to take care of their own. They formed activist organizations such as AIDS

The NAMES Project AIDS Memorial Quilt is a memorial to those who have died of AIDS. Each panel displays the names of people who died during the AIDS pandemic. It was first displayed on the National Mall in Washington, DC, in 1987.

Coalition to Unleash Power (ACT UP) in America and AIDS ACTION NOW! in Canada. Lesbians organized blood drives and cared for HIV and AIDS patients throughout North America. Svend Robinson became the first Canadian member of parliament to come out as gay in 1988, disclosing it in a televised interview during the AIDS crisis to offer hope and visibility to other members of the community.

By 2000 AIDS had killed nearly 450,000 people in the US. It's estimated that 100,524 people in Mexico died of HIV or AIDS between 1990 and 2013. Canada estimates 26,000 Canadians died during that time. The AIDS epidemic devastated gay communities at a time when society at large was not accepting of LGBTQ+ people. Much of a generation of gay men was wiped out, and many survivors still face trauma from losing friends and lovers.

Larry Nelson, an LGBTQ+ activist who lived in San Francisco during the AIDS crisis, explains it to younger generations this way: "Imagine you had a birthday party right now, and you invited all of your really good friends. You'd have ten, twenty people over, right? Imagine that group of people over a period of two years, gone. That's what it was like."

Living with HIV

In the mid 1990s new HIV treatment drugs debuted, and testing for the virus became more accessible. Improved medications allowed people with AIDS to live longer and prevented HIV from turning into AIDS. AIDS deaths finally began decreasing in the US at the end of the decade. The release of pre-exposure prophylaxis (PrEP) medication in 2012 also offered proactive protection against contracting HIV via sexual activity.

REFLECT

The COVID-19 pandemic in the early 2020s was another illness that incited a widespread response. How was the world's response to COVID-19 similar to or different from the response to the AIDS epidemic?

In 2024 there was still no cure for AIDS. But medications could help people with HIV lower their viral loads, meaning there was so little of the virus in their bodies that it was undetectable in tests and couldn't be transmitted through sexual activity.

While HIV and AIDS are no longer a death sentence if proper treatment is administered, stigma remains. Men who have sex with men faced restrictions when donating blood until the restrictions were lifted in 2023. People with HIV still can't join the military in the US, and those in Canada sometimes can, but it's determined case-by-case.

Larry Kramer and ACT UP

In the 1970s Germany's first modern gay rights organization reclaimed the pink triangle from World War II, transforming a symbol of pain and discrimination into one of liberation.

Then in 1982 as the AIDS crisis decimated gay communities in North America, gay New Yorker and writer Larry Kramer launched the Gay Men's Health Crisis. The organization shared information, fought discrimination, and provided services to AIDS patients.

As more young men died, the government's lack of urgency and aid angered Kramer. In 1987 he formed ACT UP to push for action. Eventually, Kramer's work shifted the culture around HIV and AIDS and made progress toward reducing the stigma around them. Despite contracting HIV and suffering many health problems as a result, Kramer remained an activist until his death at the age of eighty-four.

In the 1980s activists in New York City displayed posters featuring a pink upward-facing triangle and the phrase "SILENCE = DEATH" to raise awareness about the AIDS crisis. ACT UP adopted this symbol and became known for protesting and demonstrating to shift indifference.

CHAPTER FOUR
Changing Tides

By the 1990s awareness of LGBTQ+ people and the challenges they face was finally increasing. Not all representations of these challenges were positive, though some showed compassion. For example, 1993's movie *Philadelphia*, starring Tom Hanks, was the first movie to directly portray the AIDS crisis in a compassionate way.

Despite improvements, LGBTQ+ people in North America still had few legal rights and faced social discrimination. Although most US states didn't have marriage equality—the ability for same-sex couples to marry—some began offering civil unions for same-sex couples, which provided some legal benefits in those states. But since they weren't legal marriages, the federal government didn't recognize them. And the couples couldn't access the over one thousand spousal rights and benefits that come with legal marriage, including everything from tax breaks to legal protections.

Public perceptions toward LGBTQ+ people were shifting, and advocates for LGBTQ+ rights pushed for marriage equality. But the US Congress passed the Defense of Marriage Act in 1996. This law federally defined marriage as between a man and a woman, which allowed states to continue banning marriage equality.

REFLECT

Who gets to make and remove laws, and why does it matter who is put in those positions?

In 2003 Massachusetts became the first state to legalize marriage equality, with the first wedding taking place in 2004. Other US states soon followed. In 2005, two years after Ontario and British Columbia became the first Canadian provinces to legalize marriage equality, the Canadian government passed legislation permitting it countrywide. Without a national law like Canada's, same-sex couples in Mexico and the US lived in a gray area. In the US, marriage was only recognized in the state where it was performed. If you lived in a state that didn't have marriage equality, you could travel elsewhere to get married. However, neither your home state nor the federal government considered it legal.

Left to right: Antony Porcino and Tom Graff became the first legally married same-sex couple in British Columbia, Canada, on July 8, 2003.

In Mexico, the federal government passed a law in 2003 banning discrimination for sexual orientation. Still, marriage equality didn't exist in Mexico until 2009, when Mexico City legalized it. It wasn't recognized nationally, but individual Mexican states began legally allowing it starting in 2012. Then the Mexican Supreme Court of Justice of the Nation declared in 2015 that all states must permit marriage equality, theoretically making it legal nationally. But the structure of Mexico's political system means each state still had to pass its own marriage equality laws to comply with the declaration, and some states took their time. The final state, Tamaulipas, didn't pass marriage equality until 2022.

As public opinion began warming up to the LGBTQ+ community, some discriminatory rules and policies slowly ended. For example, in 2007 Mexico's Supreme Court of Justice of the Nation ruled it was unconstitutional to discharge people from the military for having HIV.

Annette Jacobson (*above*) and partner Angela Chavez (*below*) listen during a 2013 rally in support of marriage equality in San Diego, California. There was a sense of two steps forward, one step back. Marriage equality became legal and illegal in California several different times due to disagreements between mayors, governors, state lawmakers, voters, and state courts.

REFLECT

How might you feel if you finally gained a legal right but then it was taken away?

Lawrence v. Texas

One major case, *Lawrence v. Texas*, was decided by the US Supreme Court in 2003. An old Texas law had banned gay couples from participating in certain types of sexual intimacy. Two gay men in Houston, John Lawrence and Tyson Garner, were allegedly having consensual intimacy in their private home when police entered the house due to a report of a weapons disturbance. Police found no weapons but the men were arrested and accused of breaking the old intimacy law, even though the law was not strictly enforced, and the couple was at home.

The men were convicted and lost their state appeal. The appeal went on to the Supreme Court, which decided the government can't tell people what consenting adults choose to do in their homes. This Supreme Court decision ended the Texas law and struck down similar laws in thirteen other states.

Left to right: Garner and Lawrence held a rally outside the courthouse in Houston after their court victory on June 26, 2003.

CHAPTER FIVE

Fighting to Serve

The fight for LGBTQ+ rights and equality has, in some ways, been more complicated for those in the armed forces. Military policies have often been more severe than those in the civilian world. During World War I (1914–1918), gay intimacy was illegal for service members.

Following the Lavender Scare in 1975, it became illegal to ban or fire people from federal jobs for being LGBTQ+. But in 1982 the Department of Defense issued a new policy banning homosexuality in the military. Anyone in an LGBTQ+ relationship could be discharged. From 1982 to 1993, this policy resulted in more than seventeen thousand people being kicked out of the military for homosexual conduct.

Don't Ask, Don't Tell

While campaigning for US president in 1992, Bill Clinton said he would lift the ban if he was elected. However, some military leaders and politicians pushed back once Clinton was in office. They worried lifting the ban would distract service members and impact their group cohesion and readiness to fight. Then Congress passed the Don't Ask,

Left to right: **Petty Officer Autumn Sandeen, Lieutenant Dan Choi, Corporal Evelyn Thomas, and Captain Jim Pietrangelo II handcuffed themselves to the White House fence protesting DADT in 2010.**

Don't Tell (DADT) bill. Clinton signed it into law, and it went into effect in 1994.

On the surface, the policy seemed like an improvement. People in LGBTQ+ relationships were no longer banned from serving and didn't have to disclose their identity. But they also had to keep their identity private. Under DADT, if someone thought or found out a person was LGBTQ+, they could be investigated and discharged. Anyone in an LGBTQ+ relationship had to keep it completely secret. This can be especially hard in the military, where people are often deployed for long stretches and live all day alongside their coworkers.

Additionally, when someone is married in the military, the government pays for their spouse to move around the world and live with them wherever they get stationed. Unable to marry or be out, many service members in LGBTQ+ relationships had to live separately from their partners or personally pay to move their families and hope nobody found

Obama signs the 2010 act repealing DADT.

out. Some people chose to leave the military rather than stay and try to hide.

It's estimated that over 13,400 people were discharged under DADT, losing their jobs and military benefits. In late 2010 Congress passed legislation to repeal the law, and President Barack Obama signed it that December. It wasn't until nearly a year later, in September 2011, that the DADT policy officially ended in the military.

Canada had a similar policy from 1976 to 1988, banning homosexuality among anyone serving and potential military recruits. They lifted their ban without restrictions in 1992 and released even more inclusive policies in 2010 and 2012. The 1992 lift also included transgender service members.

The lifting of DADT in the US meant lesbian, gay, and bisexual people could serve openly without punishment or discharge. However, people who were openly transgender were still banned. Supporters of the remaining ban believed openly transgender service members would distract their colleagues or that they would negatively affect security or health care. Those against the ban believed the same bias-fueled reasoning from DADT was at play. In 2015 the Obama administration initiated a study to explore how allowing openly transgender people to serve would impact military readiness and health-care costs.

The administration reviewed eighteen allied countries, including Canada, that already allowed openly transgender service members in the military. After a year, the study concluded that the US should permit openly trans people to serve. It estimated there were thousands of trans people already serving who were closeted. The administration also believed trans inclusion was necessary to retain service members and attract top talent in a changing world. In June 2016 Obama's secretary of defense announced a new policy ending the ban.

The policy rolled out over several months and only applied to those already serving. It allowed them to come out as transgender without retribution and to begin socially and medically transitioning with many medical costs covered.

In June 2017 the military was set to allow openly transgender people to join too. But on the day that new transgender recruits were to be accepted, President Donald Trump's secretary of defense pushed the new policy's effective date to January 2018.

REFLECT

Would you be able to hide a major part of your personal life from people you're frequently around? Was DADT a fair policy? Why or why not?

Trans rights activists and other human rights activists protested Trump's actions throughout his 2017–2020 presidency.

Battle for Transgender Rights in the Military

One morning in July 2017 Trump dealt a massive, unexpected blow to the LGBTQ+ community. He posted on X (formerly Twitter) that he wouldn't accept any trans people serving in the military. He claimed he consulted with military leadership, but that later proved false. The posts surprised the Department of Defense.

Many trans service members had come forward and started transitioning the year before, under Obama's administration, after assurances that they wouldn't be discharged. Now they feared the Trump administration would kick them out.

After Trump's posts, his administration scrambled to create a new policy fully banning transgender service members, which was then challenged in numerous courts nationwide. The process left trans service members and trans people trying to join the military in limbo. Top military leadership opposed this new policy, saying they hadn't been consulted and that there wasn't a problem with allowing trans service members.

The Trump administration kept fighting, and in January 2019, the Supreme Court declined to hear challenges to the administration's ban, allowing an updated version of the new policy to take effect. Trans people who had already transitioned would not be discharged. But the military wouldn't pay for any gender-affirming surgeries. Also, nobody else currently serving could transition, and no new trans people could join the military.

But change was on the horizon. Later that year, Canada released new military policies that were even more welcoming of trans troops. Then in 2021 one of US president Joe Biden's first acts in office was reversing the trans military ban. His administration released a new policy supporting service members' transitions and allowing trans people to join. As of 2024 some Republican senators are still fighting the policy without much success.

CHAPTER SIX
Marriage Equality at Last

US laws protect people from discrimination at work and in public spaces. But they only apply to legally protected classes, including race, national origin, sex, age, disability, and religion.

Under federal law, if someone tries to kick a person out of a restaurant for being Asian, it's illegal. But in some states, if it's because the person is LGBTQ+, it's still legal. The US has fallen behind other North American countries with its discrimination laws. Canada added "sexual orientation" as a protected class to its federal laws in 1996, and Mexico did the same in 2003, though some people argue that the law is not effectively enforced in Mexico.

Starting in 2015 Democrats in the US Congress tried several times to pass the Equality Act, which would update the Constitution to include LGBTQ+ people as a protected class. The House passed it in 2019 and 2021, but the Senate did not. Many cities, states, and counties passed their own non-discrimination ordinances instead, creating local protections for LGBTQ+ people.

Through the 2000s marriage equality was a confusing patchwork of state laws, with couples being able to marry

In 2001 the Netherlands became the first country to legalize marriage equality.

in one state but not being recognized as married in others. Before marriage equality passed federally, the federal government didn't recognize marriage between LGBTQ+ couples even if a state did, depriving these couples of federal rights and benefits and treating them as unwed from legal and tax perspectives.

For this reason, LGBTQ+ couples were strongly encouraged to obtain legal documents such as wills to protect their families. For example, someone could create a document designating their partner to inherit their property or make medical decisions for them if they were injured. However, not everyone could afford to pay lawyers to create such documents. And these documents only helped in certain situations.

REFLECT

What other implications can you think of for couples who are denied the right to marry? What kinds of things might they have a harder time doing or not be able to do at all?

Windsor v. United States

In 2013 the US Supreme Court heard *Windsor v. United States*, which challenged the 1996 Defense of Marriage Act. Edie Windsor and her partner, Thea Spyer, had lived together for forty-four years in New York City and considered themselves engaged for forty. Spyer was diagnosed with multiple sclerosis in 1977, becoming increasingly debilitated over time.

Eventually, marriage equality became available in some states, but not theirs. They married in Canada in 2007, and while they couldn't marry in New York, the state recognized their Canadian marriage. But the federal government didn't. Spyer left her apartment and belongings to Windsor. Federal law says people don't owe estate taxes on property their spouse leaves to them. Since federal law viewed the couple as legal strangers, Windsor received a federal estate tax bill of $363,000 on Spyer's property.

Windsor sued the government. Her case went to the Supreme Court, which ruled in her favor that parts of the Defense of Marriage Act were unconstitutional and discriminated against LGBTQ+ couples by not giving them federal protections and benefits that married couples are entitled to.

The Supreme Court ruling knocked down the Defense of Marriage Act, but it didn't mean marriage equality had to be legal everywhere. Laws still varied state-by-state, which made it complicated when someone moved from one state to another. But it meant if an LGBTQ+ couple got married in a state with marriage equality, the federal government also had to recognize that marriage.

Windsor's case changed the lives of military couples too. Soon after the act fell, the Department of Defense announced it would provide all spousal military benefits to same-sex couples if they got married in a state that allowed the marriage.

Windsor was an activist and regular attendee of Pride events until her death in 2017.

Jim Obergefell

By the mid-2010s the Defense of Marriage Act fell, and the US federal government recognized marriage between LGBTQ+ couples in states that allowed them. More states were proactively changing laws to allow marriage equality, and others were forced to allow them after being successfully sued for discrimination. In 2015 more than 70 percent of states, plus Washington, DC, had marriage equality. But what about LGBTQ+ couples who lived in other states? Or what if a couple got married in a state that allowed the marriage but then moved to a state that didn't?

Enter Jim Obergefell. This gay man from Ohio met his partner, John Arthur, in 1992, and they spent twenty-two years together. Arthur was diagnosed with a degenerative condition called amyotrophic lateral sclerosis in 2011. Upon the Defense of Marriage Act ending in 2013, the pair wanted to marry, but Ohio still hadn't legalized marriage equality.

As Arthur's illness worsened, travel became increasingly difficult. Marriage equality existed in Maryland by then, so family and friends helped them charter a medically-equipped plane. Arthur and Obergefell married in the plane on the tarmac in Maryland. After returning to Ohio, they learned their state wouldn't recognize their marriage. This meant that when Arthur died, Obergefell wouldn't be listed on his death certificate as his spouse.

Obergefell v. Hodges

Arthur and Obergefell had sued Ohio for discrimination in 2013. After Arthur died, Obergefell kept fighting, and *Obergefell v. Hodges* went to the Supreme Court. On June 26, 2015, the court ruled that due to the Fourteenth

Obergefell holds a photo of Arthur as he speaks to the media after the *Obergefell v. Hodges* ruling.

Amendment's Equal Protection Clause, a state cannot deprive LGBTQ+ couples the liberty to marry. In other words, all states had to allow marriage equality and recognize all out-of-state marriages.

This ruling also helped LGBTQ+ couples with children. Many LGBTQ+ couples have children through adoption or fostering, a sperm or egg donor, or a surrogate pregnancy. Or they might raise a child that one of them had from a prior relationship. The parent—or, in some cases, both parents—had concerns that without a legal marriage, they couldn't be their child's legal guardian and would lack important rights such as the ability to make emergency medical decisions for their child. Obergefell's victory helped ensure that they could.

CHAPTER SEVEN

Progress vs. Backlash

Decades ago, it was a huge deal if a celebrity came out as gay or if there was a bi character in a TV show. And the trans community was almost invisible. Social media didn't exist yet, and there were few transgender people or characters in popular media. Those who did appear in books, movies, or other media were often ridiculed, called bad names, or worse. When people can't see themselves represented, especially positively, it can make it even harder for them to understand and articulate their identity and imagine a positive future for themselves.

Transgender Visibility

There were occasional outliers in representation, such as RuPaul Charles, who hosted a talk show in drag in the 1990s and began hosting a popular drag competition reality show in 2009. But trans culture turned a corner with the emergence of Laverne Cox. The Black transgender actress played a trans woman on a hit Netflix show starting in 2013. This role was the first time many Americans saw a positive and complex representation of a transgender person in the media.

Time magazine featured Cox on its cover in 2014, declaring transgender rights "the next civil rights frontier."

In 2015 Cox toured many colleges and universities, sharing her personal story and advocating for the transgender community through her talk, "Ain't I a Woman: My Journey to Womanhood." Cox said that growing up, she was often beaten up by other children and scolded by adults. She said that going to college and moving to New York helped her find transgender role models. "I was eventually able to accept them [other transgender people] and ultimately myself. I believe this can be the journey for each and every one of us. If we have misconceptions about people who are different from us, if we just get to know these people as people, I believe all these misconceptions will melt away."

Cox was the first openly trans person to be nominated for an Emmy Award. In addition to her acting career, she is an LGBTQ+ activist and award-winning producer of documentaries on transgender lives.

Black LGBTQ+ Representation

Recent years have seen many Black LGBTQ+ performers and artists who, while candid about the realities of racism, transphobia, and homophobia, also showcase Black joy and excellence. Prominent Black LGBTQ+ North Americans are, like Laverne Cox, breaking barriers and gaining visibility in mainstream media.

Billy Porter: The award-winning singer, actor, and fashion icon starred in a TV show about New York City's ball culture. Porter is a gay man and LGBTQ+ advocate and activist.

Janelle Monáe: This nonbinary and pansexual performer and singer is outspoken about racial justice and LGBTQ+ rights.

Jeffrey Bowyer-Chapman: This gay, biracial model, actor, and activist has starred as a queer character in multiple movies and TV shows. He was a judge on the first season of a Canadian drag competition show.

Lena Waithe: This actor, screenwriter, and producer uses her platform to uplift queer Black women. She was the first Black woman to win an Emmy for Outstanding Writing for a Comedy Series.

Lil Nas X: This rapper and songwriter was the first openly gay man to win a Country Music Association Award. The Trevor Project, an organization that seeks to end suicide among LGBTQ+ youth, awarded him for his advocacy around mental health and suicide and his openness about and celebration of his own identity.

Another person leading the way to more transgender visibility is Dylan Mulvaney, who has documented her transition and life on TikTok. Mulvaney's "Days of Girlhood" TikTok series has more than one billion views. One of her missions is to challenge preconceived notions surrounding gender identity. Through her content, she has become an advocate for transgender issues and helped start conversations about LGBTQ+ acceptance and inclusivity.

Visibility and representation for trans people have continued to grow. And there's been an increase in books, shows, and movies that more accurately depict the LGBTQ+ community. Some examples include the movie *Love, Simon* in 2018 and the TV show *Heartstopper*, which began airing in 2022 and was based on a graphic novel series of the same name.

Other parts of the community that were rarely visible before have also begun to be represented more in media. Alice Oseman's 2018 young adult book *Loveless* features asexual characters. Celebrities such as Sam Smith (*pictured*) have come out as nonbinary.

Legal Struggles

With new visibility comes new scrutiny. LGBTQ+ people have always been in society, just often in the shadows for safety. Increased LGBTQ+ representation and access to information has helped more people find the courage to live authentically at a younger age. But more younger people coming out has also meant more backlash against LGBTQ+ people, especially in the US.

Legal struggles have brewed between those with opposing beliefs, such as between people with differing religions and between those who are religious and those who aren't. For example, while public opinion polls show most Americans support LGBTQ+ rights more than ever, many conservative lawmakers hold religious beliefs in conflict with this. They push for anti-LGBTQ+ laws despite a lack of public support because they believe religious freedom justifies discrimination against LGBTQ+ people. But critics of these laws argue that religious beliefs shouldn't hold ground in legal conversations because the US is supposed to have a separation of church and state. Plus, LGBTQ+ people impacted by the laws may not share the lawmakers' beliefs, so some people argue that it isn't fair for LGBTQ+ people to be subjected to harsh laws based on those beliefs.

As of 2023 various states have proposed and passed a record-breaking number of anti-LGBTQ+ bills. A little over one hundred state bills targeted the LGBTQ+ community in 2018. By the end of 2023, more than five hundred had been proposed nationwide that year.

REFLECT

Should lawmakers be allowed to ban certain groups from actions such as marriage or military service if the lawmakers' personal or religious values don't align with them? Why or why not?

Two thousand people gathered outside the Iowa State Capitol on March 5, 2023. They rallied in support of LGBTQ+ rights and to oppose the anti-LGBTQ+ bills advancing through the legislature.

These discriminatory laws disregard facts and medical experts. For example, they claim transgender youth often undergo surgery to medically transition (most don't) but don't realize that many intersex youth still undergo nonconsensual surgeries, often as babies. Some laws have banned diversity and inclusion efforts in local government and colleges. Others target students in grade school. Many bills specifically target trans and nonbinary youth. Others aim to curtail classroom discussions and books involving any LGBTQ+ people. Some have banned activities or resources such as gender-affirming care, transgender student participation in sports, the use of

Many families participated in the National Trans Visibility March in Sacramento, California, on October 9, 2021.

affirming pronouns for trans students, books with LGBTQ+ characters or topics, and drag shows.

The lawmakers who write and advocate for these bills have claimed affirming practices and LGBTQ+ people themselves are corrupting young people, forcing their identities onto them, and even making them LGBTQ+. They failed to realize more kids are coming out as

LGBTQ+ not because they were indoctrinated, but because they have more information, support, and representation in media than older generations.

Many proposed bills ultimately don't pass, but those that do are incredibly harmful for the targeted populations. Because of that, many who support the LGBTQ+ community have urged schools to support and protect LGBTQ+ students and have advocated against anti-LGBTQ+ legislation.

Conservative Canadian politicians have also started advocating for banning transgender-affirming health care and LGBTQ+ discussions in classrooms. All the US and Canadian legislative efforts and harmful rhetoric around being LGBTQ+ have led to an increase in violence and discrimination against LGBTQ+ people in North America, especially against transgender people. Some LGBTQ+ individuals or their families have even left their homes and moved to states or regions where they feel safer. In June 2023 the massive US LGBTQ+ advocacy organization Human Rights Campaign declared the first-ever national state of emergency for LGBTQ+ people in the US. In Canada, LGBTQ+ and allied lawmakers have vocalized concerns about backsliding LGBTQ+ rights, especially with a rise in anti-LGBTQ+ protests and conservative politicians trying to pass discriminatory laws mirroring those in the US.

Biden and Canadian prime minister Justin Trudeau have repeatedly spoken out against these laws and have enacted various policies and programs to support the LGBTQ+ community. But if courts or legislative bodies do not make the policies law, future leaders can still reverse them.

CONCLUSION

You Can Be Part of the Change

In 2024 more North Americans identified as LGBTQ+ than ever. There's hope in the fact that so many more young people identify as LGBTQ+ than older generations. As being out and open grows more common, there's an opportunity for more people to understand LGBTQ+ issues and change their views on supporting laws that would harm people in that community. Hopefully over time, as people better understand the LGBTQ+ community, members of the community will face less legal and social discrimination.

The LGBTQ+ community is strong, resilient, and more visible than ever, but it also needs allies to help achieve full and lasting equality. Together, LGBTQ+ advocates and allies can push back when they hear someone misgender a person or say something discriminatory. They can contact their lawmakers when those lawmakers make decisions that deprive LGBTQ+ people of their rights. And advocates and allies can help educate their loved ones about LGBTQ+ issues.

With enough compassion, information, and visibility, it's likely that over time, the world will continue to become a safer, more equal place for the LGBTQ+ community.

Be a Changemaker

If you want to play a role in making the world a better place for LGBTQ+ people, what can you do? Here are some ways to get started:

Vote! Once you turn eighteen, register to vote and cast your ballot for candidates with platforms that support LGBTQ+ rights.
Contact your lawmakers. Even if you're not old enough to vote, you're still a constituent of your area's senators and representatives. If someone who represents you is proposing or supporting anti-LGBTQ+ bills, contact them to voice disagreement. Politicians have official websites, and you can use their contact form or email if you don't want to call.
Volunteer on campaigns. Volunteer for a candidate in your area whose platform affirms LGBTQ+ rights. There are many easy ways to get involved, such as campaigns where you call or text voters.
Support local LGBTQ+ organizations. Research to see if any organizations in your area are run by or support the LGBTQ+ community and see what opportunities are available. There are often volunteer roles in everything from helping set up events to mentorship to collecting donations.
Get involved at school. See if your school has any LGBTQ+ organizations for the community and allies that you can get involved in. If not, consider helping start one.

A CDC study released in 2023 found that about 25 percent of US teens identify as LGBTQ+.

GLOSSARY

activist: someone who actively campaigns for social or political change, often by participating in protests, demonstrations, or other forms of direct action

advocate: to support or argue for a cause or policy. An advocate is one who supports or promotes the interests of a cause or group.

Allied powers: a group of countries (United States, United Kingdom, Soviet Union, China, and France) that worked together during World War II to fight against the Axis powers (Germany, Italy, and Japan)

ally: a person who supports, stands up for, or provides assistance to an ongoing effort, activity or struggle. An LGBTQ+ ally supports and stands up for the rights, dignity, and equality of LGBTQ+ individuals.

ball culture: a subculture within the LGBTQ+ community, particularly among Black and Latine individuals, where they express themselves through dance, fashion, and creativity. Individuals compete in pageantry events called balls where they showcase their talents, style, and identity.

discrimination: a prejudiced or biased outlook, action, or treatment

dogma: a set of beliefs that a group of people accepts without question

Equal Protection Clause: a part of the US Constitution's Fourteenth Amendment that ensures that all people are treated fairly under the law. This clause helps guarantee that everyone has the same rights and opportunities, regardless of background or identity.

exile: a forced absence from one's country or home

gender identity: a person's internal sense of their gender, such as being a man or a woman, a combination of both, or neither

Hijra: a person from India who was registered as male at birth but who identifies as female or as neither male nor female

homophobia: a fear of, aversion to, or discrimination against LGB people

indoctrinate: to teach someone a specific set of beliefs, influencing their opinions, attitudes, or perspectives and usually discouraging questioning of those beliefs

Māhū: individuals in Hawaiian culture who embody both male and female traits or characteristics. They may identify as third gender or may not conform to traditional male or female gender roles.

marginalized: a social or economic process where individuals or groups are pushed to the edges or margins of society and excluded from the mainstream

marriage equality: the legal recognition of marriage between individuals regardless of their gender or sexual orientation. It ensures that all couples have the same rights and responsibilities regarding marriage.

misgender: to refer to or address someone using a pronoun or gendered language that does not align with their gender identity

Muxe: an individual from the Indigenous Zapotec culture in Mexico who is assigned male at birth but whose gender representation may combine both masculine and feminine characteristics. Muxes often identify with and are seen as a third gender.

orientation: a person's emotional, romantic, or sexual attraction to people

out: to reveal someone's hidden or confidential information, particularly their sexual orientation or gender identity, often against their will or without their consent

stigma: a set of negative and unfair beliefs that a society or a group of people have about something

third gender: a person who identifies as neither a man nor a woman and one who is not transitioning

transition: the process of making changes to align one's gender identity to their outward appearance and how others perceive them. Medically transitioning is to have medical interventions to alter one's physical characteristics. Examples include hormone therapy or gender-affirming surgeries.

trauma: a term used to describe deeply distressing or harmful experiences that can have lasting effects on a person's mental or emotional well-being

Two-Spirit: a term some Indigenous North American peoples use to describe a person with both masculine and feminine qualities, beyond the gender binary of man and woman

SOURCE NOTES

14 "Soon the day . . . hatred and ignorance.": Eric Marcus, "Magnus Hirschfeld," Making Gay History, podcast audio, 2019, https://makinggayhistory.com/podcast/magnus-hirschfeld/.

19 "We were tired . . . it was illegal.": Neal Broverman, "Don't Let History Forget about Compton's Cafeteria Riot," *Advocate*, August 2, 2018, https://www.advocate.com/transgender/2018/8/02/dont-let-history-forget-about-comptons-cafeteria-riot.

25 "Intersectionality is a . . . of these things.": "Kimberlé Crenshaw on Intersectionality, More than Two Decades Later," Columbia Law School, June 8, 2017, https://www.law.columbia.edu/news/archive/kimberle-crenshaw-intersectionality-more-two-decades-later.

28 "Imagine you had . . . it was like.": Emily Starbuck Gerson, "Larry 'Lare' Nelson: On Living through the AIDS Pandemic and Being a Dedicated Volunteer," Profiles in Pride, April 27, 2018, https://profilesinpride.com/larry-lare-nelson-on-living-through-the-aids-pandemic-and-being-a-dedicated-volunteer/.

47 "I was eventually . . . will melt away.": Emily Aronson, "Actress and Activist Cox Talks about 'Journey to Womanhood'," Princeton University, November 18, 2015, https://www.princeton.edu/news/2015/11/18/actress-and-activist-cox-talks-about-journey-womanhood.

SELECTED BIBLIOGRAPHY

Adkins, Judith. "These People are Frightened to Death: Congressional Investigations and the Lavender Scare." National Archives, *Prologue Magazine*, Vol. 48, No. 2, Summer 2016. https://www.archives.gov/publications/prologue/2016/summer/lavender.html.

Cheves, Alexander. "9 LGBTQ+ People Explain How They Love, Hate, and Understand the Word 'Queer'." *Them*, June 14, 2023. https://www.them.us/story/what-does-queer-mean.

Clarke, Mollie. "'Queer' History: A History of Queer." National Archives, February 9, 2021. https://blog.nationalarchives.gov.uk/queer-history-a-history-of-queer/.

Human Rights Campaign. "The Journey to Marriage Equality in the United States." Accessed January 18, 2024. https://www.hrc.org/our-work/stories/the-journey-to-marriage-equality-in-the-united-states.

Moon Cronk, Terri. "Transgender Service Members Can Now Serve Openly, Carter Announces." US Department of Defense, June 30, 2016. https://www.defense.gov/News/News-Stories/Article/Article/822235/transgender-service-members-can-now-serve-openly-carter-announces/.

Rhude, Kristofer. "The Third Gender and Hijras, Hinduism Case Study—Gender." Harvard Divinity School. Accessed May 15, 2024. https://rpl.hds.harvard.edu/religion-context/case-studies/gender/third-gender-and-hijras.

Rothberg, Emma. "Marsha P. Johnson." National Women's History Museum. Accessed May 15, 2024. https://www.womenshistory.org/education-resources/biographies/marsha-p-johnson.

Steinmetz, Katie. "The Transgender Tipping Point." *Time*, May 29, 2014. https://time.com/135480/transgender-tipping-point/.

US Department of Defense. "Don't Ask, Don't Tell Resources." Accessed January 20, 2024. https://www.defense.gov/Spotlights/Dont-Ask-Dont-Tell-Resources/.

Yale University Library Online Exhibitions. "We Are Everywhere: Lesbians in the Archive." Accessed January 18, 2024. https://onlineexhibits.library.yale.edu/s/we-are-everywhere/page/lesbian-aids-activism.

FURTHER INFORMATION

Books

Caldwell, Stella. *Pride: An Inspirational History of the LGBTQ+ Movement*. New York: Penguin Workshop, 2022.
This exploration of the LGBTQ+ movement dives into the rich history and milestones that have shaped the LGBTQ+ community. The book covers key events, people and struggles, challenges, and triumphs, including pushes for equality and the legalization of marriage equality.

Dawson, Juno. *This Book Is Gay*. Naperville, IL: Sourcebooks Fire, 2021.
This informative guide covers a wide range of topics related to LGBTQ+ identities, relationships, and history. It also includes real stories from people across the LGBTQ+ community.

Prager, Sarah. *Queer, There, and Everywhere: 23 People Who Changed the World, 2nd Edition*. New York: HarperCollins, 2023.
This book explores the lives of twenty-three LGBTQ+ individuals who made significant contributions throughout history. From ancient times to the present, this book highlights the diverse stories of LGBTQ+ people who have shaped the world.

Vaid-Menon, Alok. *Beyond the Gender Binary*. New York: Penguin Workshop, 2020.
This book dives into the complexities of gender beyond the binary. It provides an insightful exploration of identity, challenging societal norms, and advocating for a more inclusive understanding of gender.

Wind, Lee. *The Gender Binary Is a Big Lie: Infinite Identities around the World*. Minneapolis: Zest Books, 2024.
Using primary sources such as first-hand accounts and news stories, Wind explores various cultures and their understandings of gender, highlighting the existence of multiple genders beyond the binary framework. This book challenges the traditional notion of gender, gender roles, and identities, arguing that they are socially constructed concepts.

Websites

Advocates for Youth—LGBTQ Youth Resources

https://www.advocatesforyouth.org/

Advocates for Youth provides comprehensive resources on sexual health, rights, and justice. Their LGBTQ+ youth section includes articles, toolkits, and information addressing the unique needs of LGBTQ+ teenagers.

Gay, Lesbian and Straight Education Network

https://www.glsen.org/

The network works to create safe and inclusive schools for LGBTQ+ students. Their website provides resources, educational materials, and information on creating a supportive school environment.

Human Rights Campaign

https://www.hrc.org/

The campaign's Youth and Campus Engagement webpage provides information on LGBTQ+ issues, advocacy, and resources for young activists. It empowers young people to get involved in promoting equality.

National Youth Advocacy Coalition

https://www.nyacyouth.org/

This coalition is dedicated to advocating for and with LGBTQ+ young people. The website offers resources, tools, and information on issues affecting LGBTQ+ youth, empowering them to advocate for LGBTQ+ rights.

Queer Kid Stuff

https://www.queerkidstuff.com/

Queer Kid Stuff is an online resource that creates LGBTQ+ educational content for young people, including videos and articles that cover a range of LGBTQ+ topics accessibly.

The Trevor Project

https://www.thetrevorproject.org/

This organization provides crisis intervention and suicide prevention services for LGBTQ+ youth, along with educational resources.

INDEX

ABOUT THE AUTHOR

Emily Starbuck Gerson is a writer from Houston, Texas, but she currently lives wherever her wife's military career takes them. She is an award-winning journalist who has written for numerous national publications. Her areas of expertise include human interest, LGBTQ+, caregiving, military, and personal finance. When not researching or writing, she loves making art and embroidery, reading, traveling, and relaxing with her wife and rescue dogs.

PHOTO ACKNOWLEDGMENTS

The images in this book are used with the permission of: © blvdone/Adobe Stock, p. 5; © Alessandro Biascioli/Adobe Stock, p. 7; © o_a/Adobe Stock, p. 8; © GL Archive/Alamy Photo, p. 11; © Klaus-Dietmar Gabbert/picture-alliance/dpa/AP Images, p. 13; © United States Holocaust Memorial Museum, courtesy of Magnus Hirschfeld Gesellschaft, p. 14; © United States Holocaust Memorial Museum, courtesy of National Archives and Records Administration College Park, p. 15; © New York Public Library, p. 17; © Yalonda M. James/AP Images, p. 19; © Steve Edreff/Shutterstock Images, p. 20; © Patsy Lynch/Alamy Photo, p. 21; © TCD/Prod.DB/Alamy Photo, p. 23; © lev radin/Shutterstock Images, pp. 24, 43; © Library of Congress, pp. 25, 27; © Directphoto Collection/Alamy Photo, p. 29; © RICHARD LAM/AP Images, p. 31; © ZUMA Press Inc/Alamy Photo, p. 32; © MICHAEL STRAVATO/AP Images, p. 33; © Pablo Martinez Monsivais/AP Images, p. 35; © Chuck Kennedy/National Archives and Records Administration, p. 36; © Rachael Warriner/Shutterstock Images, p. 38; © supamotion/Adobe Stock, p. 41; © UPI/Alamy Photo, p. 45; © DFree/Shutterstock Images, p. 47; © Geoffrey Clowes/Shutterstock Images, p. 49; © Michael F. Hiatt/Shutterstock Images, p. 51; © Chris Allan/Shutterstock Images, p. 52; © Tint Media/Shutterstock Images, p. 55.

Cover Photo: © Watsamon/Adobe Stock

Design Elements: © Ezhevika/Shutterstock Images